DRAWING MADE FUN

DRAW ANYTHING YOU LIKE

Robin Lee Makowski

Rourke

Publishing LLC

Vero Beach, Florida 32964

www.rourkepublishing.com

All illustrations Robin Lee Makowski.

Editor: Frank Sloan

Cover design by Nicola Stratford

Library of Congress Cataloging-in-Publication Data

Makowski, Robin Lee.
 Draw anything you like / Robin Lee Makowski.
    p. cm. -- (Drawing made fun)
  ISBN 1-59515-470-1 (hardcover)
 1. Drawing--Technique--Juvenile literature. I. Title. II. Series.

 NC655.M35 2006
 741.2--dc22

2005014996

Printed in the USA

CG/CG

Rourke Publishing
1-800-394-7055
www.rourkepublishing.com
sales@rourkepublishing.com
Post Office Box 3328, Vero Beach, FL 32964

INTRODUCTION

Remember when your friends could ride a two-wheeler and you couldn't? Then you practiced and learned to ride so you could ride with your friends. You may have worked hard at learning to ride your bike, but it meant a lot to you to learn, so you kept trying and you did it! It's the same with drawing.

One of the most frustrating things for me as a young artist was drawing something that didn't look the same on paper as what I was looking at, or as I saw it in my mind. I didn't know how to fix it or have anyone to help me make it better. But I worked hard and learned how to do it.

Correct drawing is a skill that can be perfected by learning about what you're seeing, then learning how to draw what you see. This is a book that, with practice, will help you to see how objects relate to one another in size, shape, placement, and light so you can draw them correctly. You will be much happier with your artwork if you read the instructions and practice.

There are easy ways to put an image on paper. Anyone can trace something someone else has already drawn or project an image and draw around the lines. It's more work to learn how to do it correctly. Once you learn, however, you'll feel as free as when you rode that bike for the first time. You'll be able to capture a scene that inspires you or to draw something from your head that people around you will recognize when they look at it.

MATERIALS

The two most common problems with drawing are not seeing how the parts of the object line up and using the wrong materials. The first problem will be solved with practice. The second problem is much easier to fix. You'll have a lot more fun and success with your drawings if you're not fighting with hard pencils, dry erasers, and thin paper.

These materials are available almost anywhere and will make your practice much easier:

Best to Use

Soft Pencils (#2B or softer)
Thick and Thin Drawing Pens
Soft White Eraser or Kneaded Eraser
Pencil Sharpener
Drawing Paper Tablet
Tracing Paper
Wax-Free Graphite Paper (helpful but not necessary)
Crayons or Colored Pencils or Colored Markers
Correction Fluid

More Difficult to Use

Typing or Computer Paper
Hard or Pink Erasers
Hard Pencils (if the pencil will mark your hand, it's soft enough)

LAYING DOWN THE LINES

You can do your preliminary drawing (and make your mistakes) on tracing paper and then transfer it to the drawing paper. If you draw directly on the drawing paper, you can keep your drawing clean by putting a piece of scrap paper under your hand so you don't smear the pencil as you work.

When you start your drawing, use light lines so you can erase. Your preliminary shapes do not need to be perfect; they are only guidelines for your final drawing. Make sure everything lines up! We'll talk more about this as we go.

Tracing paper can take a lot of erasing. To transfer your preliminary drawing, use wax-free graphite paper between the tracing paper and drawing paper. Be sure the graphite side is down! Draw back over your original drawing with a colored pencil so you don't miss transferring part of it. If you don't have graphite paper, turn over your drawing and draw with your soft pencil back over the lines. Turn it right side up; place it on the drawing paper and trace back over the lines with a colored pencil. You will have a nice, clean drawing to finish.

Intersections

Look at the drawing below (A). Look at the size of each object. Look at what's larger, what's smaller, what's closer to you, the viewer. Look at what's farther back on the table. What are you really looking at?

All there are in the drawing are lines. Different shapes, different sizes, some higher on the page, some lower. Some overlap others and some don't. But they're simply lines drawn on a two-dimensional plane (paper) to make your brain see a three-dimensional picture! How can you learn to do that?

Now look at the same picture with the intersecting lines (B). If you want to make something look closer, draw it over (in front of) the objects behind it and lower on the paper. If you want to make something look farther away, draw parts of other objects over it, make it smaller, and place it higher on the paper.

To make something look like it's on top of a table, draw the horizon line (the line where the sky and the land, or the wall and the table, meet) through the objects and not under them.

A.

Seeing the correct size and placement of each object on the paper depends on how you draw them on the paper, relating them to the other objects in the picture.

Practice drawing from the example. When you are confident, set yourself up a few objects on the table in front of you and just practice getting the placement correct. Once things are in the right proportions, you can finish your drawing (see Rendering and Tone on pages 17-19).

Tip: When setting up this grouping, don't get too complicated! Get the placement and sizes right relative to all the objects, then move them around and try again.

B.

Light source

Horizon

cereal box

orange

Glass

Bowl

Apple

Napkin

Horizon

Milk

Pitcher

Intersections - Relationships of items of plane

Perspective and Horizon

Keeping things in perspective is a good idea in life, but absolutely necessary in drawing! Perspective is the system for depicting three-dimensional objects that recede in space on a two-dimensional plane. Objects of the same size appear larger or smaller in proportion to their distance from the viewer. By following a few simple rules on perspective, you can depict this in your drawings and make them more realistic.

The horizon line is very important in any drawing. It's the point at which the sky touches the land or sea, but if you're indoors, how do you find the horizon? The viewer, or the artist, determines the horizon. It's the imaginary line across the room where the plane of your sight hits the wall. If you look up, your horizon shifts up. If you look down, so does the horizon. And it might be different for the person sitting next to you!

Objects recede, or appear to move away from you, and disappear at the horizon. If you stand in the middle of the street and look toward the horizon, the buildings closest to you are up over

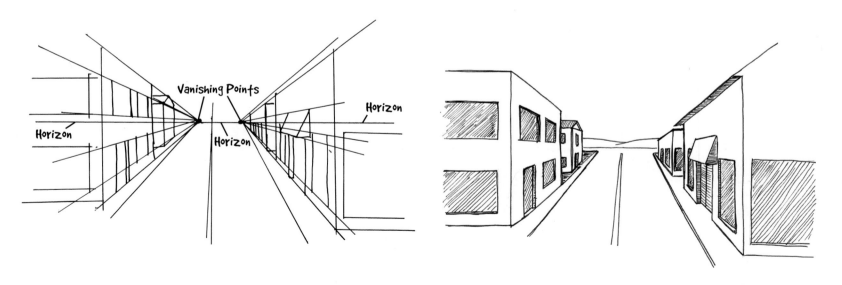

your head. The ones farthest away are lower. The point way down the street where they all disappear is the vanishing point.

Little Boxes and Cylinders

Learning how to draw boxes may seem like a boring task, but it will quickly prove challenging! Why should you learn to draw boxes? Think about it: look around the room. Look at the table. What's its basic shape? How about the chair? Can you see the box around the chair? Look at the doorway. Look at the window. The refrigerator. The desk, computer, even a car or a truck! Practice drawing the boxes from different angles and watch how perspective and the horizon line affect and interact with them.

Circles and ellipses (receding circles) are nearly as common as boxes. Use the same principles to practice drawing round boxes, or cylinders.

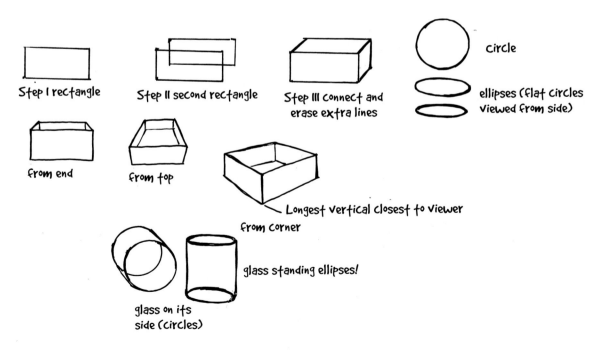

Step I rectangle

Step II second rectangle

Step III connect and erase extra lines

circle

ellipses (flat circles viewed from side)

from end

from top

from corner

Longest vertical closest to viewer

glass standing ellipses!

glass on its side (circles)

The Grid

As long as there has been drawing, there has been a basic drawing aid: the grid. The grid is used to see placement and size in a drawing more easily. You can use a grid if you have a photograph you're trying to reproduce, or if you're trying to redraw something larger.

Your source material (photograph, drawing, etc.) should be proportionally the same as the paper you're transferring it to. To enlarge an 8" x 10" photograph 200%, your drawing paper should be 16" x 20", which is two times each number.

It's best to create your grid on tracing paper and put it over your source material, but you can draw the grid directly on the source, if you prefer. Carefully measure out and draw your lines at 2-inch intervals both horizontally and vertically. You should have 4 squares wide by 5 squares high for 8" x 10".

Now take your drawing paper and do the same thing, but double the squares to 4 inches and very lightly and very carefully draw the lines on your drawing paper. You should end up with

The grid enlarging from smaller source material

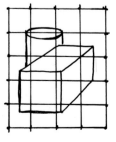

source

Enlargement to drawing paper

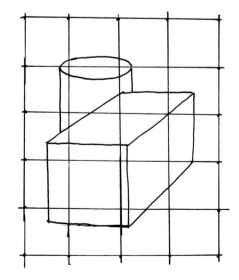

the same ratio: 4 squares by 5 squares. You will want to erase the grid squares before you finish your drawing.

To transfer your drawing, simply look at what's in each square on your source material and draw it in the corresponding squares on your grid! Keep it simple at this stage: just get the basic information transferred. Once you have it correctly, erase the grid lines and refine your drawing.

> **Tip:** Don't let the grid become a crutch! With practice, you should be able to draw just as accurately without the grid.

Sighting

Sighting is the simple method of lining objects up on a grid without the grid. Use your pencil: hold it at arm's length either straight horizontally or straight vertically to your eye. Line up objects visually and draw them from sight. This works best when drawing from life.

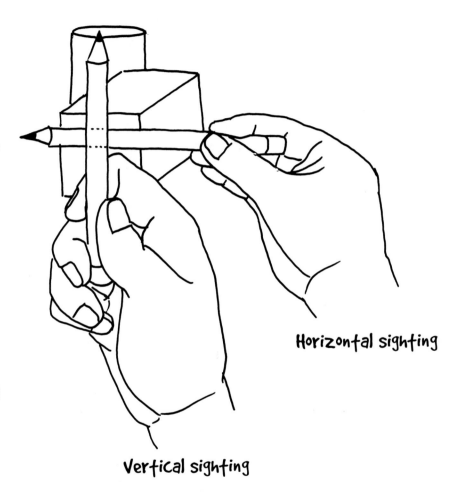

Horizontal sighting

Vertical sighting

Shapes

One of the biggest mistakes made when drawing is starting with the outline. By the time the outline is finished, the proportions are way off. Everything you draw in this book will start with larger geometric shapes to get the proportions and to get everything lined up correctly. Then the details will emerge from there.

First, study what you want to draw, and break everything down to its basic shape. Is it basically a circle? A rectangle? Most of the shapes will be based on a box or cylinder.

Pick one object to start. How wide is it compared to how tall? Get its proportions correct, then go on to the next object. What is its basic shape? Is it higher or lower on the page? Where does it intersect with the first object? Does it touch it? Where exactly does it touch? How wide and tall is it compared to the first object? Remember: at this stage, use only the simple forms. Once you have everything lined up and sized correctly, you can start rendering.

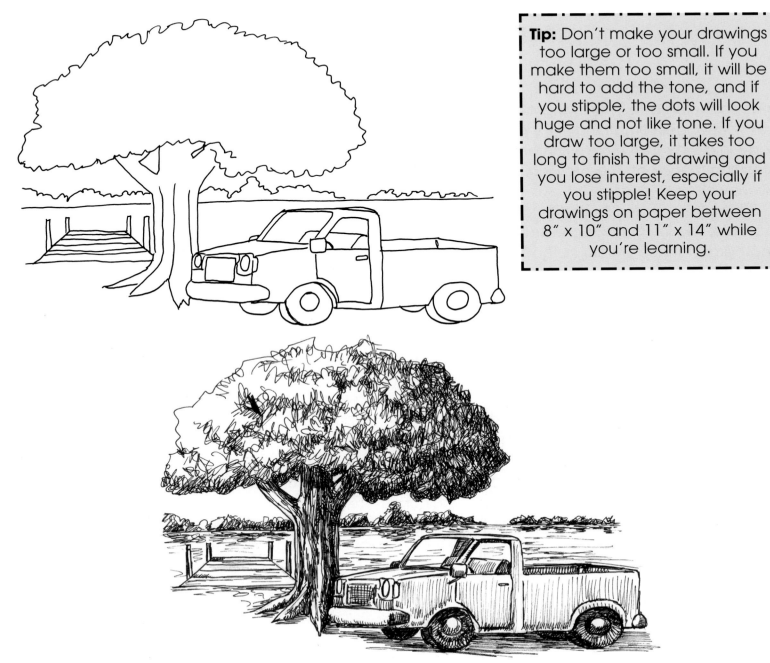

Composition

Composition is one of the most basic and important elements in drawing. No matter how well you render something, if it's not placed on the page in a way that makes it interesting or intriguing to look at, the drawing will not work for the viewer.

Look at the water lily and lily pads in the example. The image was created from a photograph taken by the author. All of the elements from the photo are in the overall drawing. Now look at the boxes. The thicker box is a horizontal composition; the thinner box is vertical. First, take some strips of paper and cover the outside edges of one box, then the other. See if you think one is stronger or more interesting than the other.

Pay attention to the path your eye takes when looking at the drawing. There should be a place where you enter, a path you move around, and a place where you exit. Most times, you go back in and look around the drawing again. This particular grouping of items will work either way, if you follow a few simple rules.

Rule of Thirds - Imagine a tic-tac-toe grid over your drawing. Is there anything centered in the box in the middle? Is it the primary subject, meaning the first thing you see when you look at the drawing? Placing anything primary directly in the center creates an unbalanced and less interesting composition. You want to place your objects above or below the horizon and left or right of vertical center. Look at the example. The water lily, the main focus, is above center in both versions of the composition.

Bleeding - Bleeding refers to drawing part of an object off the edge of the page. This creates interest: while drawing your eye to the edge of the page, your mind wonders what is going on beyond it. Bleeding indicates that the composition is but a part of what's really going on and invites the viewer to create the rest of the image in his or her mind.

Evens or Odds - An odd number of objects in the composition is more interesting than an even number. Sometimes groups of objects, like the overlapping lily pads, appear to the mind as one.

In this composition, there is one main subject, the water lily, and eight lily pads, some of which bleed off the page. This grouping creates a nice path that your eye wants to travel through and your mind can create in.

Creative License - When using source materials, try not to copy anything directly, especially if it breaks any of these rules. The most common excuse for a bad composition is, "That's how it was in the photograph!" All you're doing is taking a poorly composed photograph and creating a poorly composed drawing from it. Draw what you know and not just what you see! Use the *information* in the source material and change it to create a great composition.

Following these simple rules will improve your composition and make your drawings look professional!

Horizontal composition (box with heavy lines)

Bleed

Vertical composition (box with thin lines)

Experiment with your composition: ask a friend to look at your drawing and then explain what he or she looked at first, second, and last. "Traveling around" a drawing is subconscious: we don't think about what we're doing unless we've been trained in art, we just do it! Remember: "That's beautiful!" might stroke the ego and tell us we've done a good job, but it tells us nothing about improving our skills. Appreciate the positive comments but work toward eliminating the negative comments!

Tip: Don't draw any element too close to any border. Your eye wants to wander around the elements in a drawing. Placing something too close will not allow it to squeeze through comfortably. It adds much more interest to leave a path, or cut one off completely, around any object.

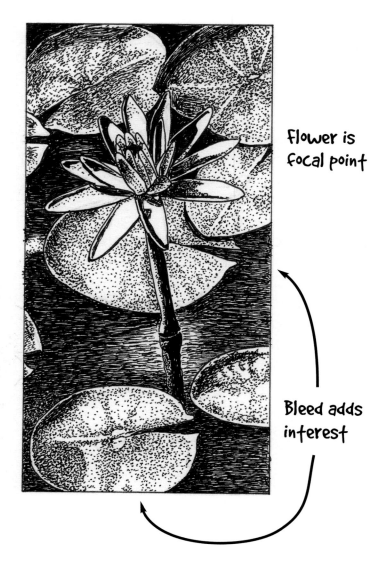

Flower is focal point

Bleed adds interest

Rendering and Tone

Once your proportions and placement are correct, it's onto the fun part: rendering. Rendering is finishing, adding detail, and adding tone (sometimes called "shading"). All this adds atmosphere and light to your drawing and, when done carefully and correctly, will bring your drawing to life.

Rendering is seeing and adding all the detail, while tone focuses on the actual color of the objects and the quality of light hitting the object. Light bounces on, off of, and around all objects. The more dramatic the light, the more realistic your drawing will be. You don't have to render every detail in an object for effect; in fact, you're better off focusing on the light, or at least equally on detail and light.

1. Crosshatching

17

Look at the same object drawn three different times. The only difference is how the object has been rendered.

1. Crosshatching and Line with Art Pen (Tone with Line). The tone is either there or it isn't. You're creating an illusion using black ink and white paper.
2. Stippling with Art Pen (Tone with Line). The same rule applies as in #1, except that the illusion appears more tonal because of the application of tiny dots.
3. Toned with Soft Graphite (Gradated Tone). This is true application of tone.

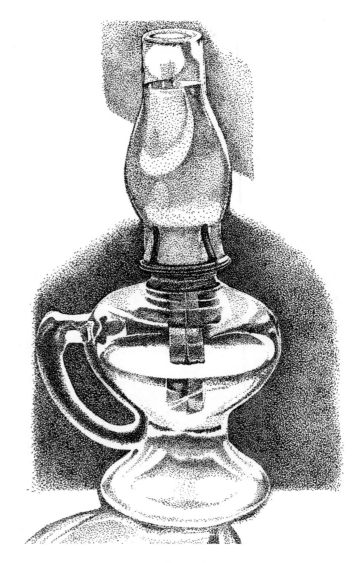

2. Stippling

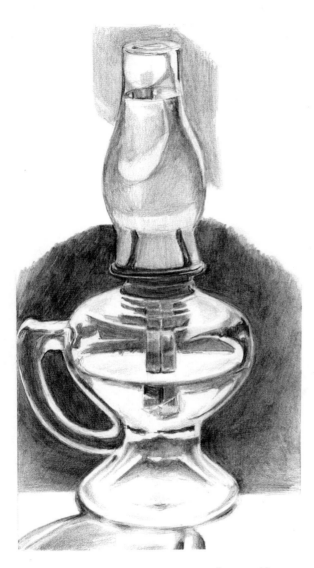

3. Graphite (pencil)

Please remember that you'll never be able to get true black with graphite. If you mix your media (ink and graphite in the same drawing), be careful! The ink will make the graphite look faded, and your eye will go directly to the place with the black ink in the drawing.

Tip: Avoid the urge to take your finger and smear the graphite! You'll get much better results if you practice applying the graphite from the pencil using different pressure in dark and light areas. It helps to have a variety of pencils that vary in hardness (H) and softness (B). Don't use a pencil harder than HB. The larger the number next to the B, the softer the pencil is and the darker you'll be able to make the tone.

Drawing Feathers and Scales

A great variety of animals have either scales or feathers. Animals with feathers or scales have hundreds of them, which can be a big job for an artist to reproduce! There are a few tricks to drawing feathers and scales.

The first thing is to look at how the scales and feathers grow. If you've never drawn scales before, the tendency is to draw a criss-cross pattern across the side of the animal. That can work if you curve the pattern instead of drawing it straight. The best way is to practice doing it correctly and to create good work habits from the beginning.

Fish and reptiles have similar scale patterns for the most part, with scale size and variation changing from the back to the belly, with larger scales on the face and head. With birds, it's different. Birds are the only animals with feathers and have many different types of feathers over their bodies.

Macaw: Start with a long, thin teardrop shape and add the head and beak shapes. The wing is represented by an oval with rows of larger feathers. There are thousands of tiny feathers on the head and breast; do *not* try to draw every tiny feather! Concentrate on the areas where the definition of each feather is more obvious. Use tone sparingly or you'll end up with a blob.

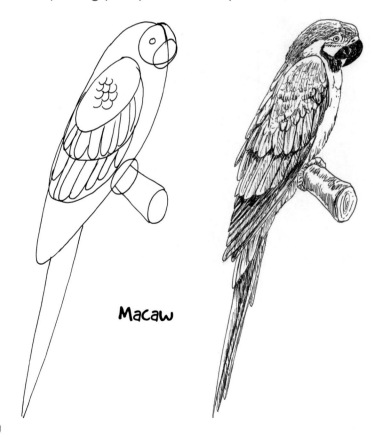

Macaw

Tarpon: Start with a half cigar shape. Define the head and add the triangular pectoral fin. The lateral line starts behind the tarpon's head and goes its length to the tail. A tarpon has large scales that are easy to draw. Start the line of scales across the lateral line. Following the example, add the scales and gill plates on the head, the mouth detail, and finish the scales.

Snake: This generic snake is a good practice subject. Start with the oval for the head and the loose double "S" shapes to indicate the moving body. Notice the placement of the eyes. Give yourself a pattern to follow by drawing curving lines down the length. Use this as a guide to add the scale pattern.

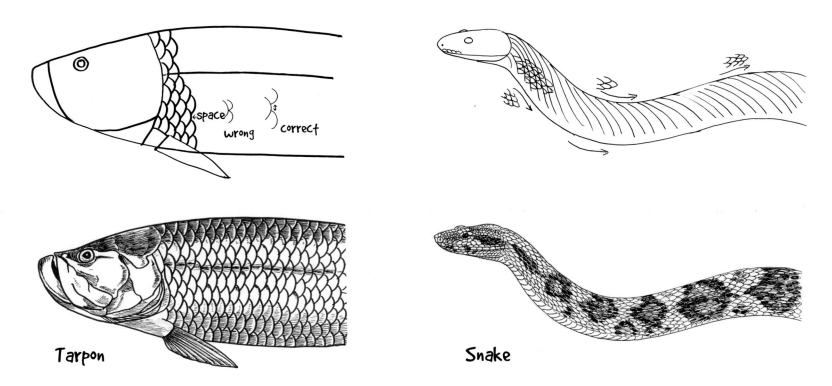

Tarpon

Snake

Drawing Fur

With a few strokes and a little practice, you can draw fur. Practice on a wolf's face, because it demonstrates lots of different lengths of fur.

Start with your basic shapes and map out the areas where the tone will change. Before you start drawing the fur, study the map that shows which direction the fur grows in on which part of the head. Notice that on the nose, the fur is very short. Use stippling for any fur that's very short. As you move to the area around the eyes, the fur gets longer. Increase the length of stroke, making certain you follow the direction the fur grows.

22

The ruff around the wolf's neck is the longest fur on the head, and beneath the head it forms tufts. Use long strokes in the direction the fur grows. You can turn your paper around and work upside down if it's more comfortable for you to make the strokes in one direction. Remember to keep a clean piece of paper under your hand and move it as you work to keep your drawing clean.

People and Figures

Drawing people is a lot less difficult than you think. There are a few things to pay attention to with people:

1. Adults are about 7+ heads high.
2. Small children are about 4 heads high. Their heads are larger in proportion to their bodies and they have shorter torsos.
3. Elbows bend at the waist.
4. Hands hang at mid-thigh when the arm is down.
5. Legs are about half an adult's height.

Find interesting poses instead of just drawing people standing or sitting. In "Boy on the Rocks," the boy is reclining and relaxed as he takes in the scenery. To draw "Boy on the Rocks:"

1. Start with your basic shapes. There are a lot of triangles in this composition.
2. Smooth out the lines and create a tone map for the clothes and hair.
3. There is a little stippling in the skin tones, but this drawing is mostly line and cross-hatching.

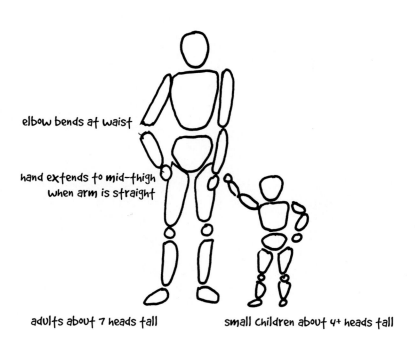

elbow bends at waist

hand extends to mid-thigh when arm is straight

adults about 7 heads tall   small children about 4+ heads tall

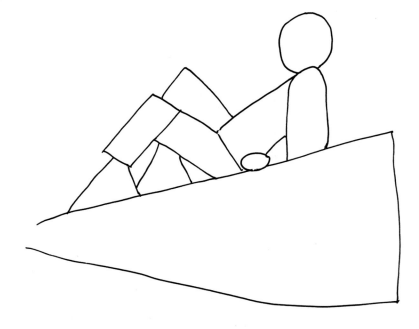

Notice how the sharp details are in the figure. Because of them, your eye goes there first. The *contrast* (difference between the darks and the lights) is strongest in the main subject, and recedes from it.

What is the boy looking at? Use your imagination!

Tip: Remember, while the drawings in this book are all pen, the preliminary guideline steps were drawn with pencil so they could be erased. Keep your preliminary lines in pencil and very light so you can erase them as you go, and use your ink over the top. You should not have three or four separate drawings showing the steps. You should end up with one final drawing that was built on pencil steps that were erased as you proceeded.

Faces

Most people are afraid to draw people and faces. The main reason is that they're afraid that viewers will say that the drawing doesn't look like the subject.

Drawing faces follows the same formula as drawing anything else. Getting a perfect likeness takes practice, but it's very fulfilling when your viewer says, "It looks exactly like him!"

Study the "formula" of the face. There are a few things to pay attention to:

1. Placement of the eyes is halfway between the top of the skull and the chin. Most often they're drawn too high.

2. Placement of the nose is halfway between the eyes and the chin.

3. Placement of the line of the mouth is halfway between the bottom of the nose and the chin.

4. There is the width of one eye between the other two eyes.

5. Placement of the ears is between the eyebrows and the bottom of the nose. Most often they're drawn too high.

6. The neck starts just behind the ears.

7. The corners of the mouth line up with the pupils of the eyes.

8. The fullness of the bottom lip starts toward the center of the lip, not in the corner.

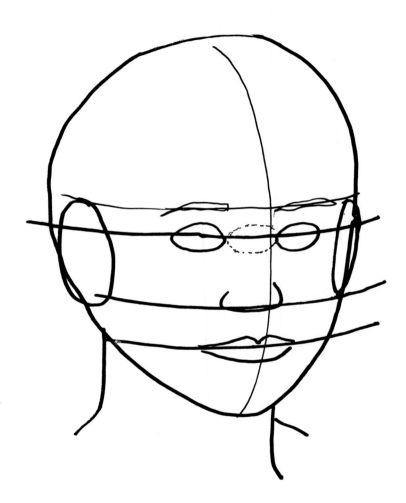

Of course, there are exceptions to every rule, but for the most part, if your drawing doesn't look quite right, check to see if everything lines up correctly (eyes too close together or far apart?)

1. To draw Matt, start with the basic shape and place all the features where they belong. Since this is practice, it doesn't matter to anyone but you if the likeness isn't perfect. Just go for a good, balanced drawing the first time.

2. Refine the drawing and get everything in the right place. Draw in a tone map so when you're adding tone, you know where to start and stop and change values.

3. Use stippling for the skin tones. It's more challenging to use stippling for the hair than line; it depends on time and dedication to your drawing. The example uses line for the clothes, but stippling looks great for fabric. Don't try to draw too much detail in the mouth or separate the teeth with lines; you'll lose it. If you plug up the teeth with too much tone, paint them back with masking fluid.

Most of all, have fun!

Structures and Foliage

Generally, when you draw some kind of a building, there will be some sort of plants around it. This drawing helps you practice composition, perspective, and application of tone. In school, you try very hard not to scribble, but in this drawing, you're going to find that it's the right thing to do!

If you've ever seen architectural renderings, when you look closely at the foliage, you'll see lots and lots of scribbling. It's a fast, easy, and effective way to render foliage.

In the example, the main focus and point of interest is the building and tunnel to the ocean. Once your eye visits the ocean, it's eager for more interesting scenery. It comes back out the tunnel and starts looking at the bushes and palm trees, and then goes back into the tunnel. This is a good path for your eye to take.

1. Start with the box and triangle shapes for the main structure. Indicate the tunnel through to the ocean. Suggest that the building is larger than what you're looking at by adding the horizontal structure to the main shape.

2. Using simple shapes, suggest the foliage, including the palm fronds. Draw in the shadow areas in the tunnel and the path leading to the tunnel.

3. Draw in the planks on the building and the round

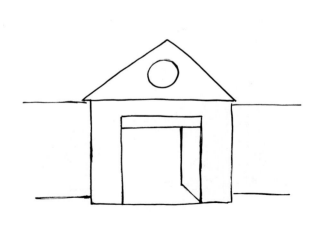

window beneath the peak. There's a great trick for drawing the window: get your circles right with your pencil, then *lightly* tone in the cross with the pencil. When you get to the pen stage, draw in the *negative space*, the space around the cross (the actual windows) with the ink. When the ink is DRY, erase the pencil and you have a perfect white cross in your window! For the foliage, the scribbling has begun…

4. Start with the darkest tone: the shadows in the tunnel, on the wall behind the palm trees, etc. Be careful in toning the ocean and the shadow in the tunnel: don't make them too close in tone!

Whatever is closest to you (the shadow) should be a little darker than whatever's farther away. Now scribble in earnest! Just like applying other tones, scribble more for darker areas and less for lighter areas. Pay attention to the direction of light (look at the shadows). Leave really light areas scribble-free. The shadows on the building from the palm fronds were lightly scribbled in, as well. Add tone to the palm fronds in the direction the fronds grow, which is from the tree out.

29

Still Life

"Still life" refers to exactly that: a scene viewed up close that won't run away from you! It can be something you set up, arrange, and control, or something you see, admire, and want to reproduce. The important thing is translating the beauty of your inspiration into an interesting, well-rendered, well-composed drawing that makes the viewer do a double take.

In the example are a grouping of the author's books and bookends. What does that tell you about the author? In this example it's obvious: the author enjoys marine life. What about changing the bookends to something you like, and maybe putting in *your* favorite books? If you showed it to your best friends, would they recognize it as "you"?

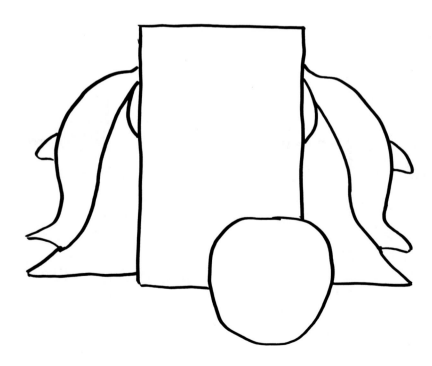

1. Start with the basic shapes. A trick for doing the bookends: use tracing paper to draw your main shapes. Detail one of the bookends. Fold the paper over so the outside edges and bottoms of the end books line up. Trace the bookend (yes, you will be tracing on the back side of the paper). Flatten out the paper and refine the rest of the drawing, making corrections to the traced bookend, as needed.

2. Add tone as needed. Use the window-cross trick on the Structure/Foliage pages to reverse out the lettering on the spines (white lettering on toned backgrounds). Decide where to stipple and where to crosshatch, or pick one and render the whole image.

> **Tip:** Take your favorite interesting objects and set up a still life with them. If you're having trouble deciding on a composition, place your objects and then leave the room for a few minutes. When you come back in, you'll have a fresh perspective. Do the same thing when you're tired of your drawing halfway through.

Conclusion

Although there's no way to cover everything in this book, there are many aspects of drawing that you will learn as you practice. Be inspired when you look at the world. Carry a small sketchbook and a pencil with you to capture moments. Write down ideas for compositions. Use the information you acquire to create new work at home. If you have a digital camera, use the rules of composition for your own photographs and use the information in them to create your drawings.

I've been drawing all my life and still enjoy it. It's a skill I'm grateful for and without which I would not be a successful artist. I know many painters who do not know how to draw, who "just want to push the paint around." They trace or project photographs and it shows in their work. The next time you go to an art festival or gallery, study the way the artists draw and paint and see if you can tell who drew and who traced.

I hope you practice and always enjoy drawing.

ABOUT THE ARTIST

Robin Lee Makowski is a professional artist, illustrator, and instructor. She specializes in watercolor painting and drawing and has illustrated more than thirty children's books.

"I always loved science and nature," explains the artist. "I studied everything closely and tried to draw it. I noticed the way things lined up, how close or far away things were, the way the light hit them, and how the light affected the color."

"It's so important to learn how to draw," she insists. "You have to realize that when you can draw, you're free. All you need is a pencil and paper and you can create wherever you are. Drawing is rewarding both in the process and the product."

Robin lives in Hobe Sound, Florida, with her husband, two sons, and her best friend, her mutt Casey.

Visit Robin at her website: www.rlmart.com